Loves Me This I Know!

JASMINE M. JOHNSON

illustrations by Samon Roy

GEMLIGHT
PUBLISHING LLC

FORT WORTH, TEXAS

Loves Me This I Know!

JASMINE M. JOHNSON

illustrations by Samon Roy

FORT WORTH, TEXAS

Copyright © 2025] by Jasmine Johnson

All rights reserved.

No part of this book may be reproduced, stored in a retrieval system, or transmitted in any form or by any means, electronic, mechanical, photocopying, recording, or otherwise, without the prior written permission of the publisher, except for brief quotations used in reviews or scholarly works.

Published by Gemlight Publishing
 Fort Worth, Texas
972.514.6705

www.gemlightpublishing.com

Cover Design by: Gemlight Media
Illustrations by Suman Roy
ISBN 9798348586232

yahuah

HEBREW NAME THAT MEANS

I Am Self Existence

Dedication

To my Dante, whose light shines ever bright. May you always remember the boundless love YAHUAH has for you.

Daniel nodded. "I know He is! He's in the water in the river that flow downstream. He's the mountain at the top standing as solid as a rock.
And if you listen with your heart, you'll feel His love too."

Suddenly, the clouds above parted, and a bright, golden light shined down through the trees. It warmed everything around Daniel and Luke. Luke gasped, his eyes wide. "What is that?"

The boys stood together in awe, looking up at the light. At the moment, they didn't feel scared or alone. They felt warm, safe, and happy, like YAHUAH Himself was giving them the biggest hug.

About the Author

Jasmine M. Johnson

Author | Storyteller | Mother

Jasmine M. Johnson discovered her passion for writing at just 10 years old, finding joy in crafting stories filled with adventure, nature, and wonder. Born and raised in Dallas, TX, she is not only a writer but also a devoted mother to an adventurous little boy who continues to inspire her storytelling.

Her debut children's book, Yahuah Loves Me, This I Know, is a heartfelt reflection of faith, love, and self-worth. She chose her son as the inspiration for the main character, Daniel—a child full of light, joy, and curiosity. Through her writing, Jasmine hopes to touch the hearts of children from all backgrounds, reminding them of their unique value and the special place they hold in our Creator's eyes.

When she's not writing, Jasmine enjoys reading, spending quality time with family, and creating meaningful moments that reflect the beauty of faith and love.

www.ingramcontent.com/pod-product-compliance
Lightning Source LLC
LaVergne TN
LVHW072115060526
838201LV00011B/243